Poetic

Conversation

Bent but

D1509871

Doris Ann Carey

12058 NC Hwy48
Whitakers, NC 27891
Dacarey49@gmail.com

Table of Contents

Acknowledgments

In my darkest hours, these poems were
birth with tears in my eyes.
So much hurt, pain, and sorrow in the depths of my soul
My marriage and family falling apart
yes me grasping for a new start
by yet not finished with the old How could this grown
woman be trapped by a bruise little girl ever be able to rise?

A life full of obstacles, hurt, and shame, barring
blame that almost left me insane.
As you travel on this poetic journey, you will see this
broken little girl evolve into this bent woman,

Through much prayer, tears, never given up the
fight determined to follow a divine light,
A light that would never let me give up the fight; even
though I was bent, life would not break my sister's circle
Whose love and guidance have been my
example of what women can overcome.
They are the ultimate role models, most importantly,
my dear friends Minister Patsy Dismuke,
Co-Pastor Deborah Dean, last but not least Prophetess
Sharon Whitfield, provided unending encouragement.
 Now, here's my poetic story of bent but
not broken, victim to victory.
Risen in God's Glory.

The Birds Outside My Window

I opened my window to my surprise
I heard the birds singing an unsung song

Most of them were in harmony gathered along the grass
The only thing that stood between us was the window glass

It felt like they were singing to me in their unique way
Oh, how they sounded like a chorus so beautiful and strong

It was the most amazing unsung song
So many birds as far as I could see

They were eating and singing so intensely, yet they
 were free
In my soul, I longed for the feeling to be me

I thought if I could only join them but, they would
Run from me

It wouldn't be the first time I got left behind this window
was my friend
The song had a melody straight from heaven they sound
so free

As I sit behind the glass, I yearned to be set free from
All I endured

Full of guilt, hurt, and shame, I realize how bound
I felt inside, always in a shadow, trying to hide

I heard a voice speak softly to me.
There are only a few things
differently between you and them.

These birds have faith in me where I
take them; they trust I will be
They fly openly singing new songs, traveling to their destiny

You are free, can't you see? It's the
windows you've created that
divides you from me

You're going to get your wings so you
can fly. I sent the birds so
that you could see I have the power to set you free

Mirror

Who is this I see? Is this the real me looking
back at me?

Tired and scared, no confidence, within
I see just a helpless woman looking back at me

Life has beaten me up. I've gotten stuck
I pray to God to show me to me

Lord, I'm blinded by the path I need to follow.
I there's an urge to just wallow in giving up seems
easier.

I'm afraid to look in the mirror can't recognize
who's looking back at me?
So tired of carrying this load being there for
Everyone else taking a toll.

Lord, I got so tired I didn't know what to do
I helped friend's, neighbors, even strangers.
Those was the instructions you gave us to do
I pushed didn't know where to turn

Am I losing my mind going insane?
No one to talk to how could I explain

I tried hard to say I'm weighted down
knew I wanted to be close to you
Starring in the mirror again. What did I see?

I saw this strange woman staring back at me
I stepped a little close, trying to recognize her.

Tears streaming down my face, God,
help me then I sat on my bed looked
to the sky.

These words I heard go to the mirror
let me tell you who I see.
I see a purpose filled woman who looks just like me.

God Can I talk to You

I started my conversation with hey God,
this is your child. I need to talk to you.
Lord, I'm hurting and angry, you see, when

I think I'm doing right. It ends up wrong
I'm afraid I feel so alone, like I don't belong.

Sad more days than I care to share,
I can hardly hold my head up just need
a touch from you.

I've fallen in a pit; I hate to admit Satan's
on my tracks, trying to hold me back.

He is trying to destroy a catastrophic attack
Literally trying to snatch my life from your
plans

 I render myself to you as I go in prayer
There is one like you to compare

Insecure and Unsure

Who am I? What do you see?
Am I whole, or is it a shell of me?

Lost in myself, trap no way out,
Nothing able to come in, nothing
able to go out.

Scared of myself, afraid of the dark
that's inside. No one to talk to seems
like an unending ride

Scared to dream, feeling no hope inside
Pain so deep, like a vast ocean tide

So much hurt, pain, that want subside.
Is this all I'm worth? There has to be more
to my birth. This feeling of being insecure
and unsure

Then one day a friend appeared she shouted,
 evident God is near
He is the Savior for the confused and
misunderstood.
Jesus is the light in our darkness days if
we trust his way

He holds the keys. He will unlock the doors
he knew you before you were born
knew your name; he created you with
purpose in mind

He created your destiny no one could fulfill,
On the cross, Jesus paid the bill.

Then she walked up to me, took my hand,
bowed on our knees started to pray
Suddenly this light, opened up my heart.

I felt God's love for it was his grace, impart
Never again to feel insecure and unsure
He promised never to depart

Fearful Love

Fearful love so cold and cruel it took over my mind, body and soul.
Constantly having to guess about fearful love could it mean this or stand for that?

Fearful love makes you stay when you should leave, hold
On to the mess you perceive.
Fearful love will make you second quest, make you lose your rest. Maybe I should hang in there a little bit longer. It may build me stronger.

I can't lose all that I have; what will
my friends and family say.
They don't care; they just want to have their way
Fearful love makes you weak. It keeps
you hoping and wishing

You can't get contentment; just keep
on fishing years of living with
fears. Some many days and nights of hidden tears. Scared of
losing what I never had, living a life of
misery, hurt, and sadness.

Losing so much time in this fearful love praying to the father
to help you from above. Oh, Jesus is
all I can say I know it has
to be a better way. Lord, what is this you're telling me to do?

Let it go turn it over to you. This fear
has a grip on me, help me
to break free.
I surrender to you all my trust in thee.
I place fear under my feet;
the devil is a liar the battle is won you
have been utterly defeated

Unspoken Touch

Have you ever been to a place?
So dark and filled with disgrace

The first time they invaded your space
Or what about that unspoken touch?

When your insides collapsed, and your heart raced
When you were scared to close your eyes

Because you kept seeing their face
Sneaking in and out of your room

Like a thief in the night to fulfill their delight
When the door opened, and you desperately
grip your sheets

Trying to act like you were in a deep sleep
Have you ever stayed up all night lying in the dark?

Praying to God to intervene and expose the unseen
Was it not bad enough that you knew your predator?

I had to see them every day, and words couldn't
form to say getaway
I know it was hard, and the pain was severe

One thing I can assure you, it wasn't in their hand
God didn't forsake you.

He has a plan to use all the pain you suffered
at night to be a testimony of his light.

Hiding Behind Secrets

Holding my pain inside, putting on a mask
of happiness
Sorrow, I try to hide loving hard, getting nothing
in return

Heartache so bad feels like I will burst and burn
Hiding my tears of life disappointments, and trials

Secrets, I can't share so many pains. I just bear
I put on my face a great big smile, trying to keep
walking and praying every mile.

People in and out of my life leave secrets of their
own.
Some bad and some many different people, same
old secrets.

If you heard it, once you've listened to it twice. I've
Learned when you see people smiling, everything
might not be is alright.

They were just carrying some hidden secret in
their hearts
Knowing at any moment if revealed, it can tear
their life apart.

You're not My Friend

Open your eyes, can't you see? The mistakes you made
the price you paid.
Instead, you worry about what I have said or how I've
gotten ahead.

I have always been there through thick and thin.
looking out for what I thought was my friend.
The minute I turn my back, you stick the knife deep
with so-called friends.

The same ones that creep like a snake bringing
bones and taking scraps
O
You so fake try to pull others down so you can
create your glory.

Deep within you, scared to death, someone may
reveal your story.
It's not new you've repeated this behavior with
other friends. They left because of your bad aura.

My heart hurts for you, and yet I'm still furious,
just curious why are you so full of insecurity?
I guess it speaks to your life and immaturity.
Why do you live in so much obscurity?

Go ahead, dig your ditches and toss your stones.
You never realize how many true friendships you've
blown.

Now tell me, how does it feel to be so empty and alone?

When It's Over

Situations lead you to know it's over and
through.
You've done all you can do, your faith been
tried and true

The process of being taken in and out of hurt,
sorrow and pain.
Hoping that it will rain to erase the stain of
misery.

The pressure makes you want to scream
and hollow.
The fight turns into intolerance separate rooms
Diminish conversations dwindles to hello and
goodbye

Tears won't come, but you want to cry
you know you gave everything
Unanswered prayers, or so you think

Go to a place of silence called the secret closet
keep praying. God hears your heart
He already knew the end from the start

In your tomorrow there will be no trace
Forgotten tears and heartache no more
God will give you permission to walk out
the door.

Lies Brought Me Out

Born into confinement, then hear the question why?
I was transported to and from, feeling a total of none.

Defending myself was never an option, though
presented as an offense.
Even when blended, I was left unattended like
the poster child or misfit.

Found with bruises and scars of lies tucked within.
How could this little girl be so bound up she was ordained?
Nevertheless to drink from this cup

I could never clean up the lies, for they were my life.
There was so much sorrow and strife.

Lies of old that scared my face, rendering me to
unintentionally grace.
As my life went on, I discovered it how to cover with tears
running down my face.

Thanking God, he was a presence in my race, nothing else
could have ever set me free.
It was his glory at the trace of the tree. I knew somebody
cared for me.

Jesus illuminated the light in my darkness for me
to see.

There had to be light to the lies that soared
deep inside of those who told the story

I am the image created in God's truth and splendor.
The truth is now revealed: I 'm not the offender.

How Much More Can I Take

No longer proud of whom I've become
So much shame, pain, and guilt

Trying to see the woman I never knew,
Lord, I want to be close to you

Please let me see who you intended me to be,
So broken, my soul feels like it dried up and died

Stripped, searching, trying to find that better day
It has to come my weary way

So many mistakes, yes, I have sinned
Will this nightmare ever end?

I never thought this was my real identity
Just searching breathlessly for my destiny

God sees how reduced I feel
Just one touch to be healed

I know you got a plan for me
Establishing my name for the word to see

Everything I went through, you were
preparing me
My purpose is to glorify you to show others
Your word is true

Can you Hear Me?

Without words, can you hear me?
A blank stare. Can you hear me?

I can't look you in the eyes. Can you hear me?
When I don't come around friends and family anymore,
can you hear me?

I'm numb to the pain; it has no sting. Can you hear me?
My mind is eating up all my hope. Can you hear me?

I keep slipping down this dark slope. Can you hear me?
There's nothing but despair. I just need someone to care
can you hear me?

I'm screaming loud. So much to endure. Can you hear me?
So, many scars carved in my soul can you hear me?

Marks on my arms get more extensive
and deeper. Can you hear me?
Every day, I grow weaker, my voice
grows feeble. Can you hear me?

Trapped within me, invisible in plain sight, can you hear me?
God, please help me win this fight. Can you hear me?

Lord Heal Me

I got spirits that try to attack, trying to infiltrate
get me off track

Some are new, some I was born into
As life progresses, the more they want to claim
possession, In my expression

The manifestation of stolen moments, pressures,
and broken promises
Evidence of dark places and controlled spaces

Tones of spoken and unspoken words that have
no truth
Deceiver of truth, confusion, and trials set up
with a smile

Significant trauma that stole my youth but
shifted me like Ruth
Lord, bearing this cup is a heavy load, but I
must sup

You hold the healing; you're the great
physician
Lord, heal my symptom's so I can complete
my mission

Broken Cord

We broke the cord that held us together
The very one that could keep us in any weather

We lost our way, and the storm never got better
Nobody knows of the trouble behind closed doors.
we lost in our way

Publicly, we know how to display the illusion
How they saw us as the perfect couple, what a
delusion

Reuniting is so far from our wounded hearts
Too ahead to turn back from the enemy
attack

Omitting the strength of the third link
Gasping for air, clinging to hope

While going through the motion of disbelief,
How do we explain to family and friends?

The unraveling cord that held us together
has broken apart
The distance we've grown apart will never create
us an opportunity to make a new start

Giving Up the Man I See

I thought I found that man of my dreams
He was handsome, tall, and strong as a tree

Yeah, all the women wanted him
Just as fine as can be

Dived in heart wide open
No direction and no instruction

I had to win the token
Then he starts to do the unspoken

A push, then a pull, a hit, then a slap
A fine man got me hooked and trapped

I wonder why he is changing so much
He was the man with the Midas touch

Masked unveiled, I saw his face
The eyes of hate and disgrace lit up

Then one day, a friend said to me,
 I know a man full of mercy and grace

His name is Jesus. He will make an escape
Never again will I be blinded by the man I see

I now know there is only one man who can
set me free

Goodbye

It's been so many times I wanted to say goodbye
I prayed so hard to see you no more.

Not writing this to beat up on your just your eyes
were so full of yourself
The real me you could never see surviving through
so much,

The happy days will never equal sadness within,
it started like a rip, now a tare

I wanted to thank you for all the lessons each one
brought me closer to God's blessings

For every word of disrespect, it taught me
to let go of regret every put down lifted me up,
I prayed, Lord, take this cup.

So many embarrassing moments there
will be atonement living in fear every time
you were near.

Those strongholds were hard to break.
It took a lot of prayers, make no mistake

They only taught me I didn't belong; you
never showed remorse when you did wrong

God provided indeed he did everything
I thought I lost.
He gave more at a lesser cost

Your lies didn't break me; they were just
distractions
God, thank you for removing the pain of his
actions

You didn't allow it to leave a stain, I pray you
 find Jesus seeking to be a God-fearing man.

As I close this letter, I hope you better sincerely,
My goodbye letter.

Just for me

The man that God has been chosen just for me.
To encourage and protect, he will sow into me

Handpicked from the finest lineage
With eagle wings, a strong push

He soars below me when it looks like a fall
One who cheers me on when I try to give up

Never has a problem being a man that will fill
an empty cup Yes, the wind beneath my wings

He knows how to stay, how to take a stand
Strong when I am weak makes me happy
when I'm sad

A man that can stand behind me when I am in front
Who walks beside me when I need a shoulder?

He walks in front to shield me from any hurt or harm
This man of mine that loves God first in prayer he
converse

He tells the truth, never has to rehearse, keeps himself
in the place even when others try to crowd his space.
Yeah, nothing like this man of mine

So grateful God gave me his best design

When a Man Loves a Woman

When a man loves a woman, he gives all
of himself
Her partner, lover, and friend less not forget
cover

He not only protects her heart but also prays
F for her soul that she holds a story untold

Putting her first never tries to pull her down
The hero, never letting her hit the ground

She is his queen, and he is her king
Proud to show it with a ring

Unheard prayers answered from above
Blessed with the grace of God's love

Supports her finding her place while running
his race
Loving her is like loving himself full of mercy
and grace

Embracing each other, through tests together
No matter what kind of storm or unseen weather

She knows the feeling of being blessed
Rejoicing, God gave his very best

Freedom

The loss of my freedom has brought tears to my eyes
The lonely nights that I have prayed and cried

Yes, you know the space that I gave away
The one that looks like I will never see another day

A cycle has no end just keep on beginning
Try to hold down a simple conversation or to
take a hot bath

You know the language you do the math
Tired of getting up, tired of lying down,

Trying to hold another sister and me down,
You know the weak one who has nothing to say

Yeah, I know you say my fault I could've or
should've done this or that
Don't you think if I could turn back the hands
of time?

I would be free with peace of mind trying to
hold on I know God will bring me through for
he holds my freedom

Pieces

God, please fix my broken pieces scattered
along the way
The elements of shattered dreams chipped away

I seek out ease while my body trembles
of the pain
Layers of hurt rooted so deep locked away in
secret shame

A chunk here a slice has torn people just
stare for they know what to say
A deep breath I take and pray

Rather than explain, I just stay away
They will never understand it easier just to
judge
I've learned to smile while the pieces pile

Dress up what's left and play the part
There is a prize at the end of this journey

My master knows what to keep what to
lose
God has the manual to my book

He designed me his perfect creation,
In my pieces is his revelation

Pray

Everybody says pray it is going to be alright
How can I when the words won't
come out my mouth?

Great instructions, then leave me all alone
Drifting like a piece of paper in the
midst of a windstorm

Blowing here and there to and from
like a kite
My heart was heavy, and my head hung low

So glad you sit high and look low
Engaged in this place called prayer

Do I get on my knees? Or lay prostrate
on my face
God, I can't do this alone
please cover me with your grace

I need strength to run this race
Feel your power as I talk to you

Understanding why I had to be
alone.
I had to pray for what's getting ready
to happen in my life

Another Pothole While
I'm Still in the Storm

Lord, Lord, have you forsaken me another pothole
while I'm still in a storm.
I know you said my trials would make me strong.

Lord, I have to tell you it feels so wrong.
I'm trying to be brave and not break down and cry

Keep this face on, living a lie trying so hard not to
show so much pain.
I was filled with so much sorrow, guilt, and shame.

I know you got plans for me; I don't know what it
could be.
I'm so confused and perplexed look at me, God
I'm just a mess.
I'm in a place where sometimes I can't pray feel
like I could run astray.

I feel like I'm at the threshing floor just can take
no more.
My purpose you have planned my destiny your
command.

My strength comes from you prepared to stand to
testify that sometimes you will have the potholes in the
storm

God Want Let Me Fall

So, many enemies have set traps in my life,
so tangled trying to make me fall down
Life's path never-ending trail unfounded in
lies ridicule of trying.

In daily payer for God to intervene teach me
your way to give me instructions strengthen
my way today.

So, many obstacles along the way trying to make
me lose my grip.

Satan was hoping that I might trip and fall even
 hit a wall.
Unlike people, God sees and knows it all.
I might trip, but I won't fall.

Go to church seeking the Lord to move me
beyond my past.
Can't enjoy praise and worship; church folks
hiding behind their mask.

Starring whispering even rolling eyes trying
me make me fall
Who would ever think the church wasn't
safe people in there don't have any grace.

I am at the mercy of God's grace, so you keep
setting your little traps, trying to make me fall.

Yes, I may trip, but God will not let me fall

Change

Change can be good or bad; it can make some
 happy and some mad.
Even though change can give you warnings,
it can
 hit you like the dew on the morning grass.

Change can hit hard and deep. It can roll over,
or seep.
Change is like the flow of the sea or could collapse
at the Ocean's bottom.

It has no preference can consume you or me.
I don't know if I will never be ready for change.
Or the effects in which it may bring or rearrange
I just know life will change.

Indeed, as the days come and go, no matter how the
wind may blow.
Hold on tight know God is capable of changing your
darkness days into a guiding light.

Restore Me Lord

Restore me, Lord!! Restore me, my heart Is heavy
I need you Lord, so give me the strength to forgive
and heal

My trust has been abused repeatedly abused.
My kindness is weakness no means yes
This hatred that I feel goes deeper than the offense

Compounded negligent behavior do
I am the clay you are the potter where
you lead me, I will follow
you are my Shepard I shall not want.

You make me to lie down beside still waters to give me rest.
Thank you, God you are the restorer
of my soul you have made
me whole.

Sit Walk Talk

Sometimes I have to sit listen a reoccurring voice deep inside me.

Sit down, the Holy Spirit says you can get control
The answers to the questions that keep plaguing you.

Open your heart, incline your ears you are unique
I spoke to you so many times you ignored my voice

I tried so hard to redirect you from entwined places
I kept you covered in undesired spaces leaving traces.

A cycle of go you wouldn't stop so I had to let you had to ride to the end
Entrapped in the illusion of temporary fun starts within.

I hear instructions so clear as I walk with him
near
I lay aside the hurt, resentment, pain, and hate.

 Your walk should help you get to the golden gate
The walk is a narrow path to my destiny and fate.

I thank God every day that I'm not too late
His blood redeems me bringing me to the light.

I sit, walk, and talk in purpose captivated by his might.

Changing

Look at me. I'm changing, trying to find my way.
I am looking for a better me getting stronger every day.

I am taking life day by day, praying God to lead the way.
You may not be able to tell just by looking at me.

Trying hard to be a better woman, friend, mother,
and wife.
Released from pain, anger, and strife cleansed by
the blood

Redeemed by the lamb Yeah, I'm changing every day
in every way.

My Message from God

I had to break the chains off your life.
I never took anything I couldn't replace.

I wanted you to see the distractions
keeping your eyes off me.
Tried to be your God to mess up your purpose and destroy
 your destiny.

I couldn't let that be so chipped away
some unnecessary stuff.
Yes, I knew it would be tough. I never
left you, always right by
your side.
I heard every prayer, groan, and tear
covering you with my grace

It was me when the pain disappeared;
the sorrow no more your
heart was filling with joy.
I'm not through wanted to let you know the trials will never
overtake you

As you fulfill your purpose you getting
wisecracking day stay in
my word it will clear the way

 You will testify of my grace so everyone
would hear your story.
and see my glory.

Whisper

Just one whisper in all my despair
One word to heal my care setting me free
from the snare

There must be an interruption of this beat
Like an old record stuck on repeat

The more I move the sounds get dimmer
Seems like I'm all alone yet standing in a
crowd

Voices speaking words none making sense
So, I chose to remain in silence everything else
seems dense

Listening for a word soft yet fierce one that
shatters or pierce.
No one can communicate with such certainty

Purifier of what others label as dirty free
the guilty

Guarded ears my confidence I will hear your
whisper

Giving It Back

Nothing in this world belongs to us.
One of the hardest things I had to learn
and adjust

I was so deep in fear, like a bottomless pit
Seasons in my life was all an illusion

Along with being around the wrong people to living
in seclusion

It's so refreshing to see what gratefulness looks
like. Processing everything terrible is not an attack.
It was God's way of re-shaping me to give back

All losses are not lost, and all wins are not victories.
Sharing your wisdom nothing can compare

We never see the purpose in plain sight.
We must overcome, climb through hills, and fight.

While we haven't reached our destiny, our experiences
has made our faith grow.

The enormous power of God, captures all your life's
 challenges to create your testimony

So, get prepared; to tell your story for it's all about
God's Glory.,

Great Reveal

You think you know my story it looks like I'm not blessed
You don't know the author of my book he's renowned Alpha
and Omega.

Life experiences made me stress disappointments were my
test.
There were sleepless nights that took
my rest many tears I shed.

Behind closed doors God began to
erase he changed my pace
in the race.

He changed my (if) to can, scratch out my (should) to would.
Deleted my pain removed every stain
you see me doing good
you think it's a typo.

Nah!! It's just God starting a new cycle so be careful how fast
you read each page.
He's changed the plot to get you engaged some will be my
biggest critic while other's will become my greatest fan.

You think it's just another book that's the hook to prepare
you for the Great Reveal.

O'Woman that I have Made

Oh, the woman that I have made so
strong and tall.
I see you make it through it all.

So many obstacles troubles to
make you fall.
I made you just like you should be.

Your eyes to see the beauty in thee.
Mind to think for yourself.

Ears to hear my voice.
Mouth to speak, pick your choice.

Hands to build, shape, and mold.
Feet to stand to be bold declaring
my word in spirit and truth

Say it loud, Oh woman that
I have made thee to be

You are a blessed creation you see
Even though I created you from the
rib of a man.

Never forget you are an essential part of
the plan.
Equipped and fully armored with my seal.

When winds blow, you stand with zeal.

Unseen Enemy

While we think we are fighting people, Satan wants to take
us deeper int0 sorrow, sadness, and pain.

To keep our lives in strife and strain the power of the unseen
 it's debilitating stopping your tracks.

It tries to stay near to keep us in fear when times get hard,
we pray, but obstacles keep coming our way.

Hardships get more challenging, we get weaker day by day.
Satan wants us to believe God isn't faithful he's trying to kill
our purpose and derail our destiny.

Our troubles formed by the invisible
enemy has no power unless
we give it some.
Remember, the war doesn't belong
to us. It belongs to the Lord.

So, take your strength in our God, strap
up in his armor for this fight
We can't operate in our might

Jesus is near, his Holy Spirt is within
cause the unseen enemy is real.

Broken but not Unglued

Brokenness when you think you can't take no more.
That next unexpected thing happens you tumble
to the floor.

Like a thirsty ground your feelings just evaporates into time.
The heart chilled from a cold cruel world full of hatred and
Crime.

You've been hurt time and time again like a revolving door
a mat on the floor seems to get treated better than you.

Repeatedly trampled, and stumped over your heart feels
like every beat is the last.

Barricaded in your thoughts disoriented in time.
The resounding of happiness and joy so loud yet
it's so far.

All hope is gone insight, you hold to his power and might
that feeling of broken but not unglued.

Held together by God's grace when you want to fall apart.

God reminds us that he is our strength so you may have
to cry or mourn.

Don't worry if your legs bend from the weight you will never
fall.

Finally, a place that your heart slows down your mind
is made up.

Your emotions intact stronger than ever now you ban accept
cloudy days as part of the weather.

The yesterday's faded away tomorrow seems brighter.
Today you stand broken but not unglued.

Power Filled Woman

God created me to be a living testimony
See the wonders and signs of the spirit, power,
and authority.

See the woman that God has created within me
In every tragedy, there was a triumph.

In every heartache, there was healing
Every mistake was a milestone

Victory comes in all sizes and circumstances
be grateful for all life's journeys

He's coming back one day to reward those who
diligently wait.
In faith, hope, and most of all, love.

He's given me a charge to keep it's been a journey yet
filled with purpose.

      Though, I'm not finished yet, he
      has equipped me with
      all that I need.

Power filled woman, yes that's me
born with a purpose to reach
my destiny.

Doris Ann Hilton-Carey